The Joy of Pop T[

This publication is not authorised for sale
in the United States of America and/or Canada.

Yorktown Music Press / Music Sales Limited

London / New York / Paris / Sydney / Copenhagen / Madrid

Exclusive Distributors:
Music Sales Limited
8/9 Frith Street, London W1V 5TZ, England.
Music Sales Pty Limited
120 Rothschild Avenue, Rosebery, NSW 2018, Australia.

Order No. AM952776
ISBN 0-7119-7291-5
This book © Copyright 1998 by Yorktown Music Press / Music Sales Limited

Unauthorised reproduction of any part of this publication by
any means including photocopying is an infringement of copyright.

Music compiled and arranged by Stephen Duro.
Music processed by Allegro Reproductions.
Cover illustration by Gillian Martin..

Music Sales' complete catalogue describes thousands of titles and
is available in full colour sections by subject, direct from Music Sales Limited.
Please state your areas of interest and send a cheque/postal order for £1.50 for postage to:
Music Sales Limited, Newmarket Road, Bury St. Edmunds, Suffolk IP33 3YB.

Your Guarantee of Quality:
As publishers, we strive to produce every book to the highest commercial standards.
The music has been freshly engraved and the book has been carefully designed to minimise
awkward page turns and to make playing from it a real pleasure.
Particular care has been given to specifying acid-free, neutral-sized paper made from
pulps which have not been elemental chlorine bleached.
This pulp is from farmed sustainable forests and was produced with special regard for the environment.
Throughout, the printing and binding have been planned to ensure a sturdy,
attractive publication which should give years of enjoyment.
If your copy fails to meet our high standards, please inform us and we will gladly replace it.

Printed in the United Kingdom by
Caligraving Limited, Thetford, Norfolk.

A Whiter Shade Of Pale (Procol Harum) 16
Bridge Over Troubled Water (Simon & Garfunkel) 4
Candle In The Wind (Elton John) 8
Every Breath You Take (The Police) 12
Father And Son (Cat Stevens/Boyzone) 19
Have I Told You Lately? (Van Morrison/Rod Stewart) 22
He Ain't Heavy... He's My Brother (The Hollies) 25
How Deep Is Your Love (The Bee Gees/Take That) 28
Imagine (John Lennon) 31
Killing Me Softly With His Song (Roberta Flack/The Fugees) 34
Let It Be (The Beatles) 37
Love Is All Around (The Troggs/Wet Wet Wet) 40
Mr Tambourine Man (Bob Dylan/The Byrds) 43
Oh, Pretty Woman (Roy Orbison) 46
Unchained Melody (The Righteous Brothers/Robson & Jerome) 51
Up Where We Belong (Joe Cocker & Jennifer Warnes) 54
Wonderful Tonight (Eric Clapton) 62
You'll Never Walk Alone (Gerry & The Pacemakers) 58

Bridge Over Troubled Water

Words & Music by Paul Simon

Candle In The Wind

Words & Music by Elton John & Bernie Taupin

© Copyright 1973 for the world by Dick James Music Limited, 47 British Grove, London W4.
All Rights Reserved. International Copyright Secured.

Cm
— you but I was just — a kid. — Your can - dle burned — out
B♭ B♭sus4 B♭
long — be - fore — your
A♭
To Coda
E♭ Fm7 E♭
le - gend ev - er did. —
A♭ E♭ Fm7 E♭ B♭ B♭7
E♭ A♭
Good - bye Nor - ma Jean. — though I nev - er knew you — at all, —
Good - bye Nor - ma Jean — from the young man in the twen - ty sec - ond row —

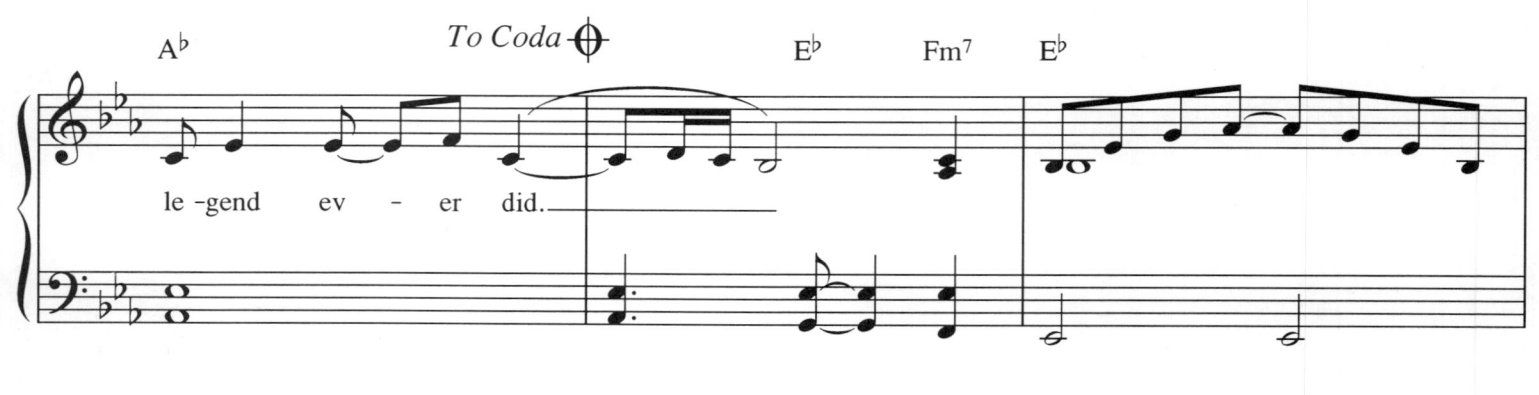

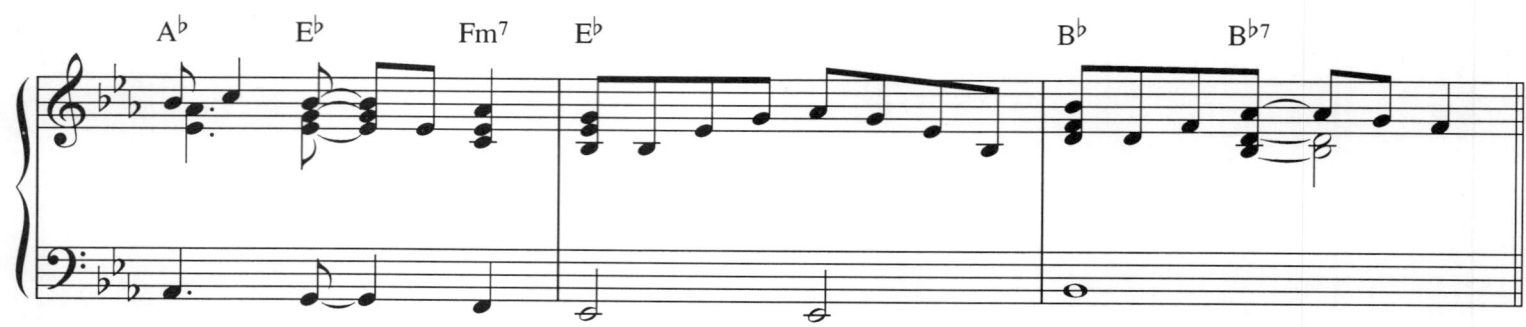

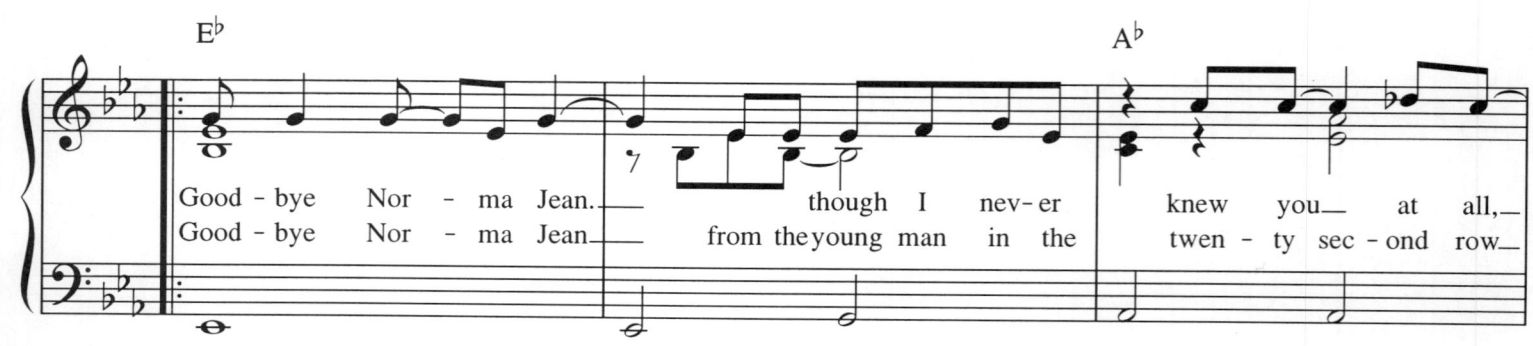

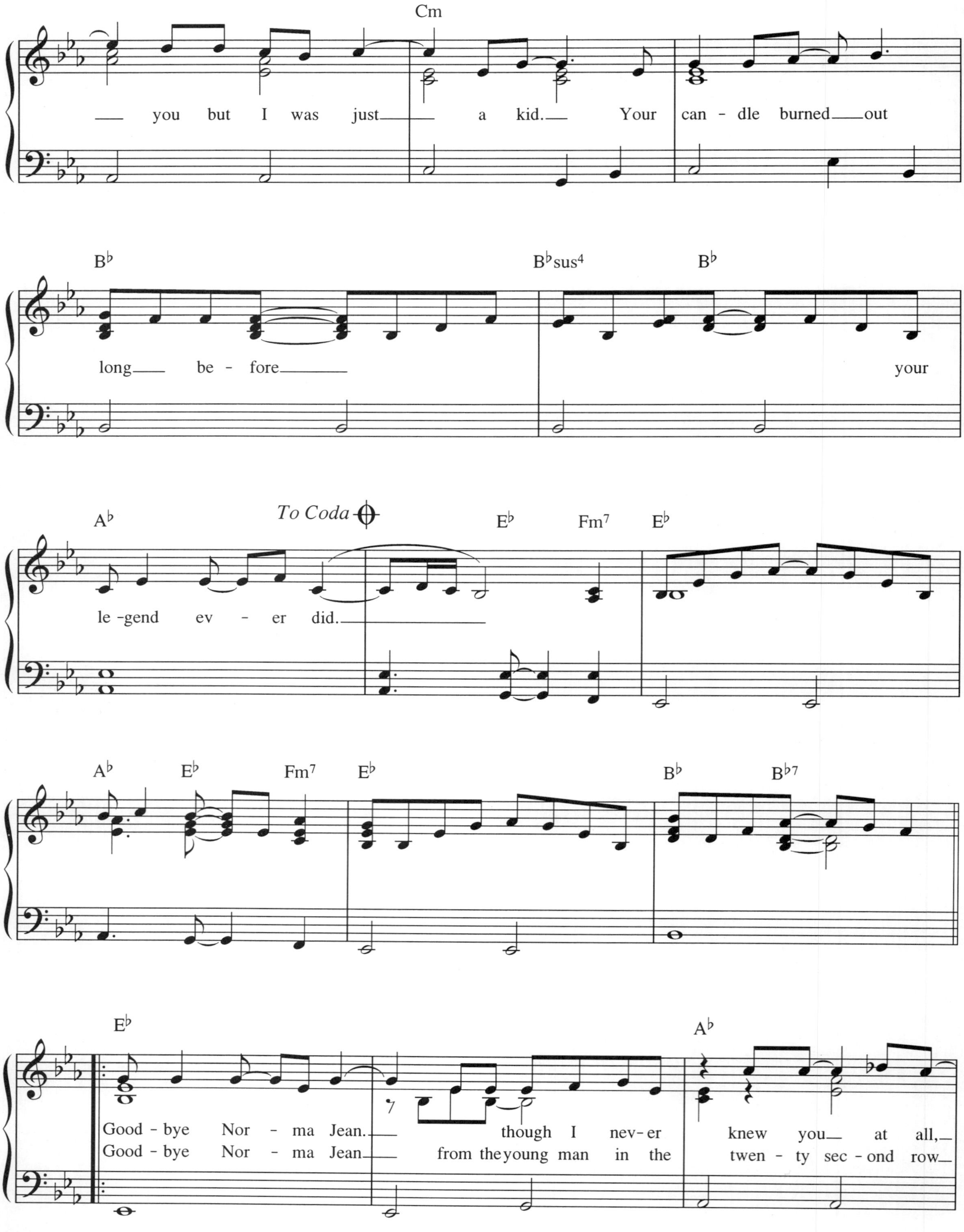

Every Breath You Take

Words & Music by Sting

A Whiter Shade Of Pale

Words & Music by Keith Reid & Gary Brooker

We skipped the light fan - dan - go And turned cart - wheels 'cross the
She said, "There is no rea - son, And the truth is plain to

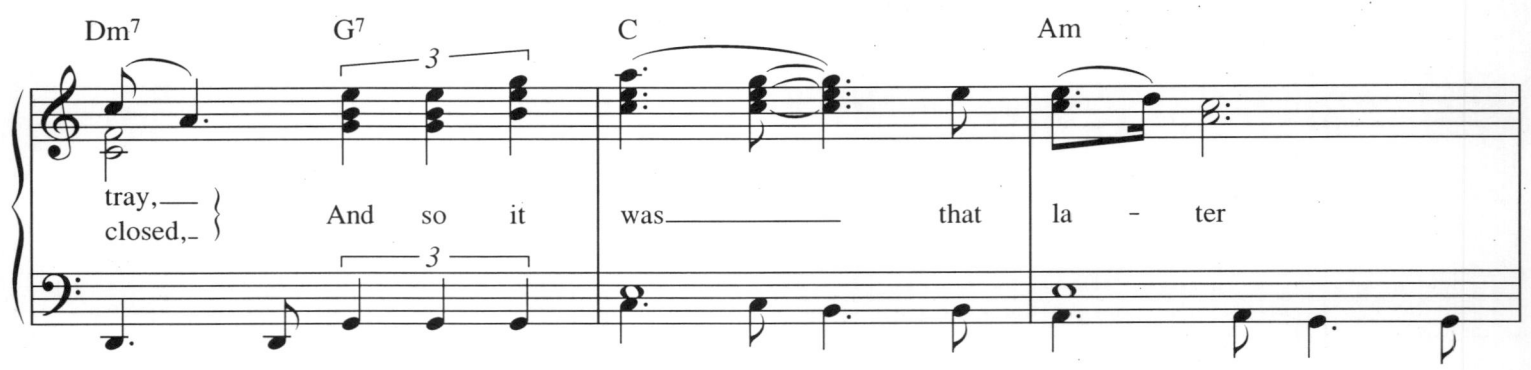

Father And Son

Words & Music by Cat Stevens

Verse 2:

I was once like you are now;
And I know that it's not easy
To be calm when you've found something going on.
But take your time, think a lot;
Think of everything you've got.
For you will still be here tomorrow,
But your dreams may not.

Verse 4:

All the times that I've cried,
Keeping all the things I knew inside;
And it's hard, but it's harder to ignore it.
If they were right I'd agree,
But it's them they know, not me;
Now there's a way, and I know
That I have to go away.
I know I have to go.

Have I Told You Lately?

Words & Music by Van Morrison

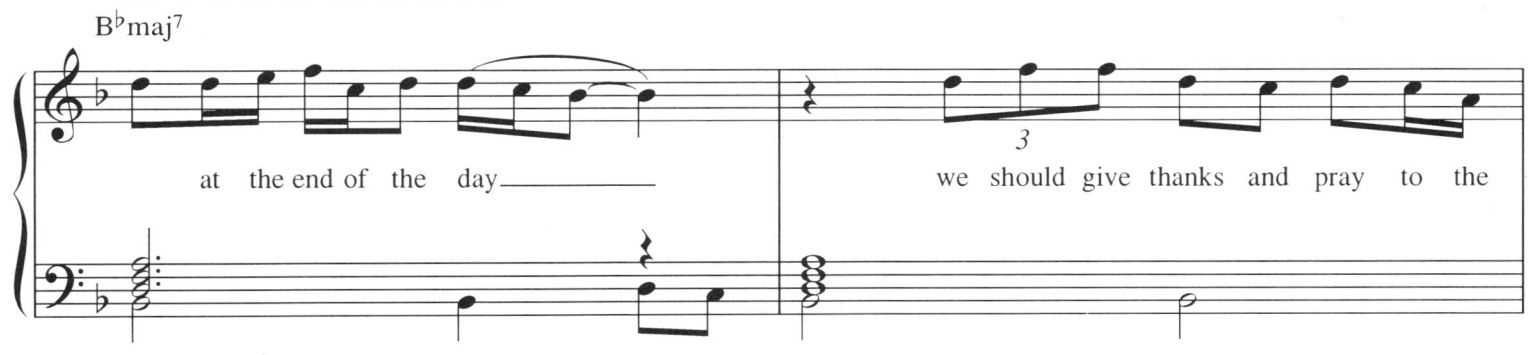
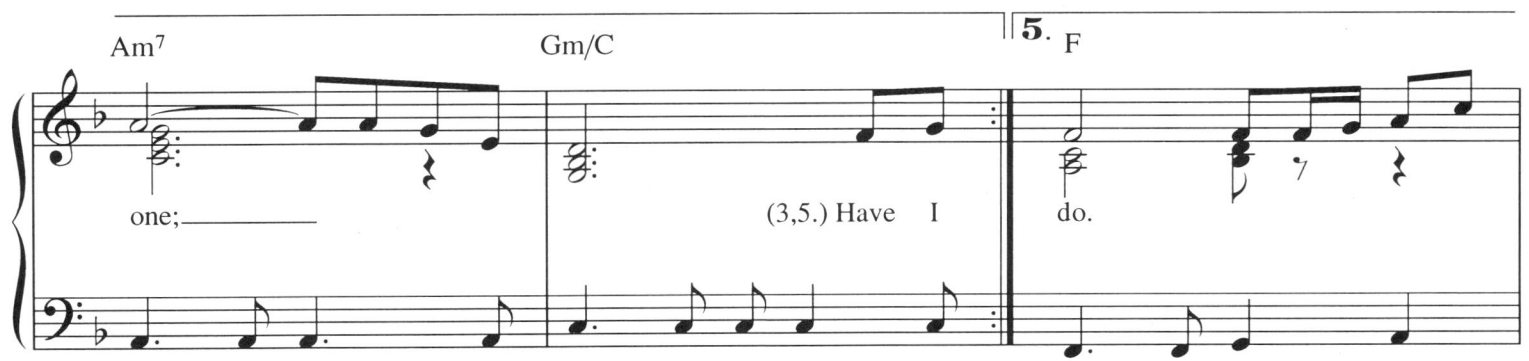

Verse 2:

Oh the morning sun in all its glory
Greets the day with hope and comfort too
And you fill my life with laughter
You can make it better
Ease my troubles that's what you do.

Verse 3: - as Verse 1

Verse 4: - Instrumental

Middle:

There's a love that's divine
And it's yours and it's mine
And it shines like the sun
At the end of the day
We will give thanks and pray to the one.

Verse 5: - as Verse 1

How Deep Is Your Love

Words & Music by Barry Gibb, Robin Gibb and Maurice Gibb

© Copyright 1977 Gibb Brothers Music.
All Rights Reserved. International Copyright Secured.

Imagine

Words & Music by John Lennon

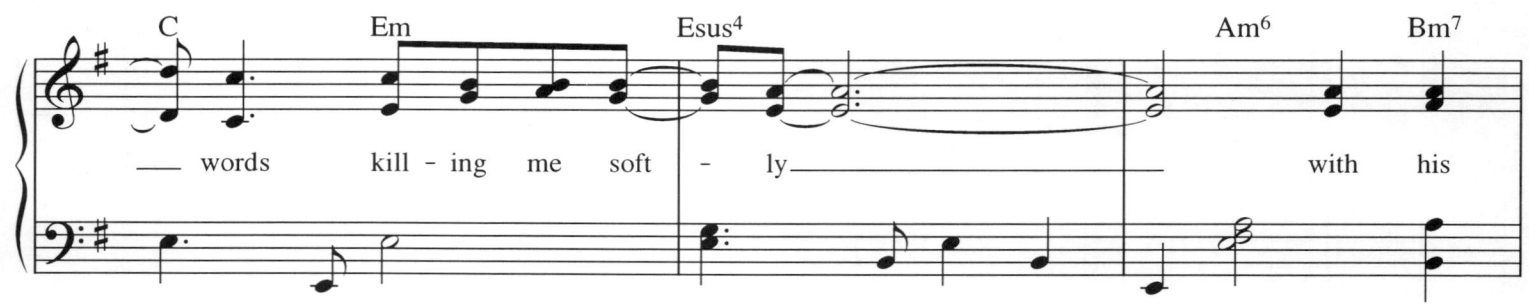

Verse 2:

I felt all flushed with fever
Embarrassed by the crowd
I felt he found my letters
And read each one aloud
I prayed that he would finish
But he just kept right on
Strumming ... *etc.*

Verse 3:

He sang as if he knew me
In all my dark despair
And then he looked right through me
As if I wasn't there
But he was there this stranger
Singing clear and strong
Strumming ... *etc.*

Let It Be

Words & Music by John Lennon & Paul McCartney

Moderately

When I find myself in times of trouble Mother Mary comes to me,
Speaking words of wisdom, let it be. And in my hour of darkness she is
standing right in front of me, Speaking words of wisdom, let it be. Let it

when the broken hearted people living in the world agree,
There will be an answer, let it be. For tho' they may be parted there is
still a chance that they will see, There will be an answer, let it be.

© Copyright 1970 Northern Songs.
All Rights Reserved. International Copyright Secured.

37

Am G F C G
be, let it be, let it be, let it be, whis-per words of wis-dom, let it
1. F C 2. F C F C G F G
be. And be.
A7sus4 A7 A7sus2 A7 D A
cresc.
And when the night is cloud-y there is
Bm G D A
still a light that shines on me, Shine un-til to-mor-row, let it
G D A Bm G
be. I wake up to the sound of mu-sic Mo-ther Ma-ry comes to me,

D A G D Bm A
Speak-ing words of wis-dom, let it be. Let it be, let it be, let it
G D A G D
be, let it be, whis-per words of wis-dom, let it be.
p
A G D A
whis-per words of wis-dom, let it be.
ff
whis-per words of wis-dom,
G D Em7 D
let it be, let it be.
3

Love Is All Around

Words & Music by Reg Presley

come on and let it show. You know I love you, I al-ways will, my mind's made up by the way that I feel. There's no be-gin-ning, there'll be no end, 'cause on my love you can de-pend.

2. I — Got to keep it mov-ing.

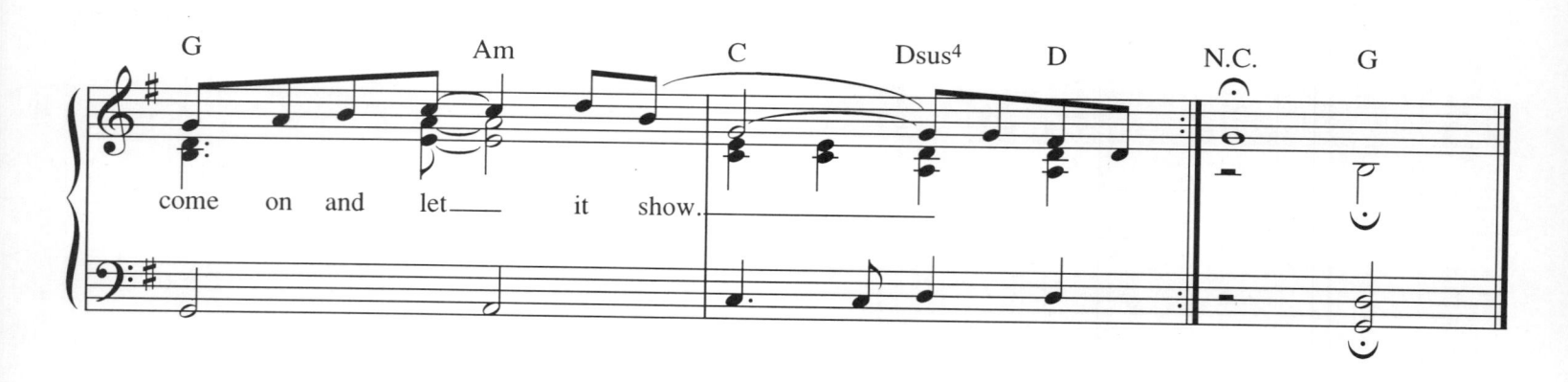

Verse 2:

I see your face before me
As I lay on my bed;
I cannot get to thinking
Of all the things you said.
You gave your promise to me
And I gave mine to you;
I need someone beside me
In everything I do.

Mr Tambourine Man

Words & Music by Bob Dylan

Moderately

Refrain

Hey! Mis - ter Tam-bou-rine man play a song for me, I'm not

sleep - y and there is no place I'm go-in' to.

Hey! Mis - ter Tam-bou-rine man play a song for me, in the

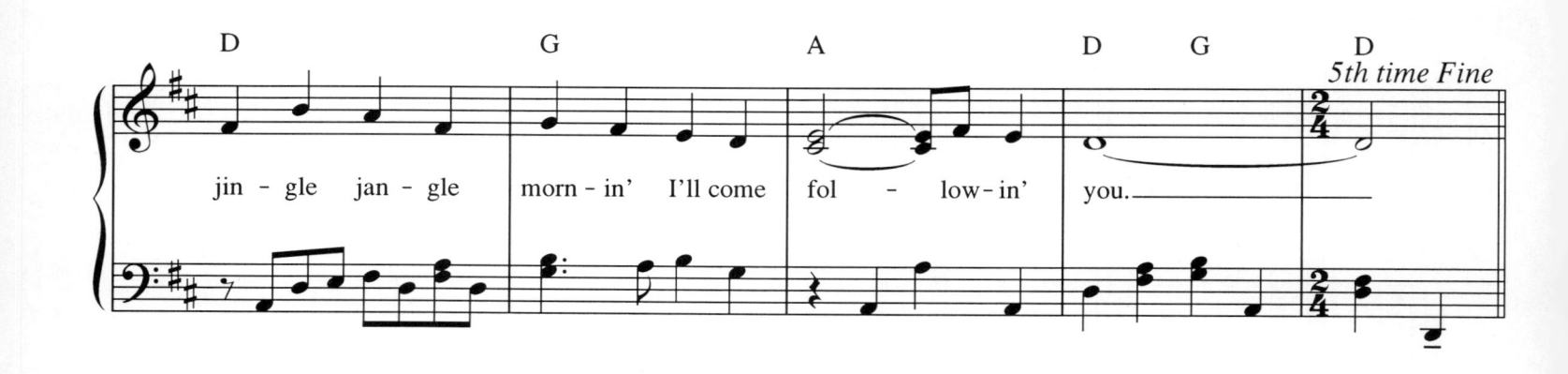

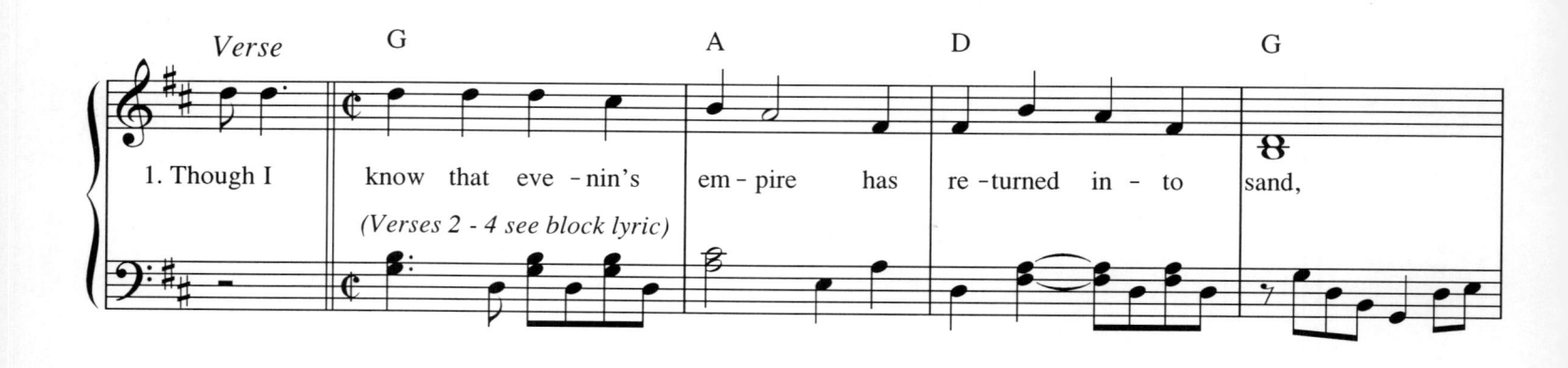

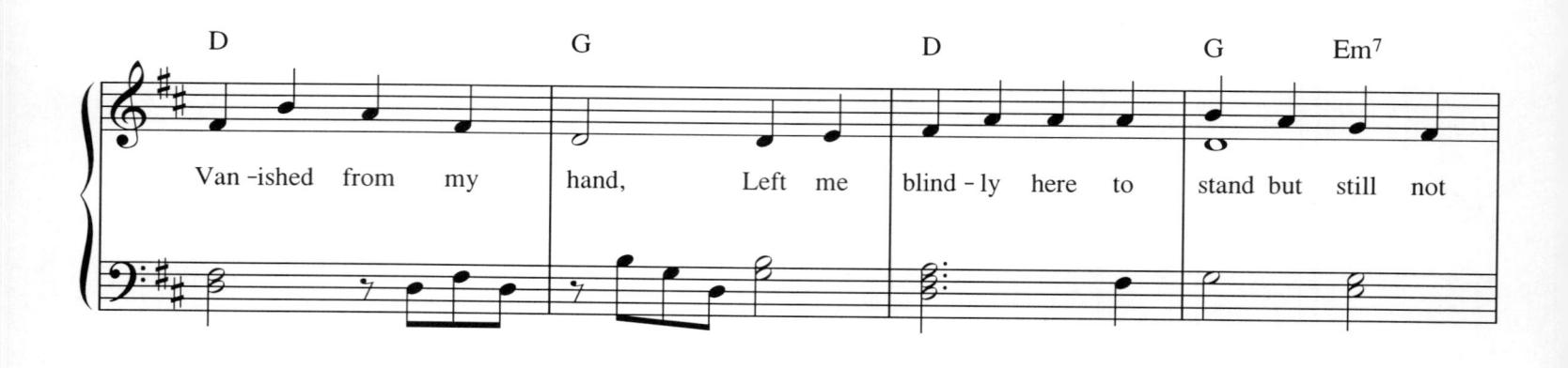

jin - gle jan - gle morn - in' I'll come fol - low - in' you.

Verse
1. Though I know that eve-nin's em-pire has re-turned in-to sand,
(Verses 2 - 4 see block lyric)

Van-ished from my hand, Left me blind-ly here to stand but still not

sleep - in'! My wea - ri - ness a - maz - es me I'm

Refrain:

Verse 2: Take me on a trip upon your magic swirlin' ship
My senses have been stripped, my hands can't feel to grip
My toes too numb to step, wait only for my boot heels
To be wanderin'
I'm ready to go anywhere, I'm ready for to fade
Into my own parade, cast your dancin' spell my way
I promise to go under it.

Refrain:

Verse 3: Though you might hear laughin' spinnin' swingin' madly across the sun
It's not aimed at anyone, it's just escapin' on the run
And but for the sky there are no fences facin'
And if you hear vague traces of skippin' reels of rhyme
To your tambourine in time, it's just a ragged clown behind
I wouldn't pay it any mind, it's just a shadow you're
Seein' that he's chasin'.

Refrain:

Verse 4: Then take me disappearin' through the smoke rings of my mind
Down the foggy ruins of time, far past the frozen leaves
The haunted, frightened trees out to the windy beach
Far from the twisted reach of crazy sorrow
Yes, to dance beneath the diamond sky with one hand wavin' free
Silhouetted by the sea, circled by the circus sands
With all the memory and fate driven deep beneath the waves
Let me forget about today until tomorrow.

Refrain:

Oh, Pretty Woman

Words & Music by Roy Orbison & Bill Dees

With a beat

Pret-ty wo-man walk-ing down the street, Pret-ty wo-man the kind I like to meet, Pret-ty wo-man_ I don't be-lieve you,_ you're not the truth_ No-one could look as good as you._ Mer-cy.

© Copyright 1964 renewed 1992 Roy Orbison Music Company, Barbara Orbison Music Company
& Acuff-Rose Music Incorporated, USA. Acuff-Rose Music Limited, 25 James Street, London W1 (50%)/
Rondor Music (London) Limited, 10A Parsons Green, London SW6 (50%).
All Rights Reserved. International Copyright Secured.

Pret-ty wo-man— won't you par-don me,— Pret-ty wo-man— I could-n't help but see,— Pret-ty wo-man— that you look love-ly as can be Are you lone-ly just like me?— Pret-ty wo-man stop a-while— Pret-ty wo-man

Fm
B♭m7
E♭7
A♭
talk a - while
Pret - ty wo - man
give your smile to
me.
B♭m
E♭7
A♭
Fm
Pret - ty wo - man
yeah, yeah, yeah,
Pret - ty wo - man
look my way
B♭m7
E♭7
A♭
F7
Pret - ty wo - man
say you'll stay with
me
'Cause I
Dm7
B♭m6
C7
F
need you
I'll treat you
right
Come to me
Dm7
B♭m6
C7
ba - by
Be mine to -
night.

F
Pret - ty
wo - man
don't
Dm
walk on by,
Pret - ty
F
wo - man
don't
Dm
make me cry,
Pret - ty
B♭
wo - man
don't
C7
walk a - way
Hey,
O.
K.
If that's the way it must be,
O.
K.
I guess I'll go on home it's late
There'll be to -

-mor - row night, but wait! What do I see?

Is she walk - ing back to me? Yeah, she's

walk - ing back to me! Oh,

Pret - ty wo - man.

Unchained Melody

Words by Hy Zaret
Music by Alex North

Moderately

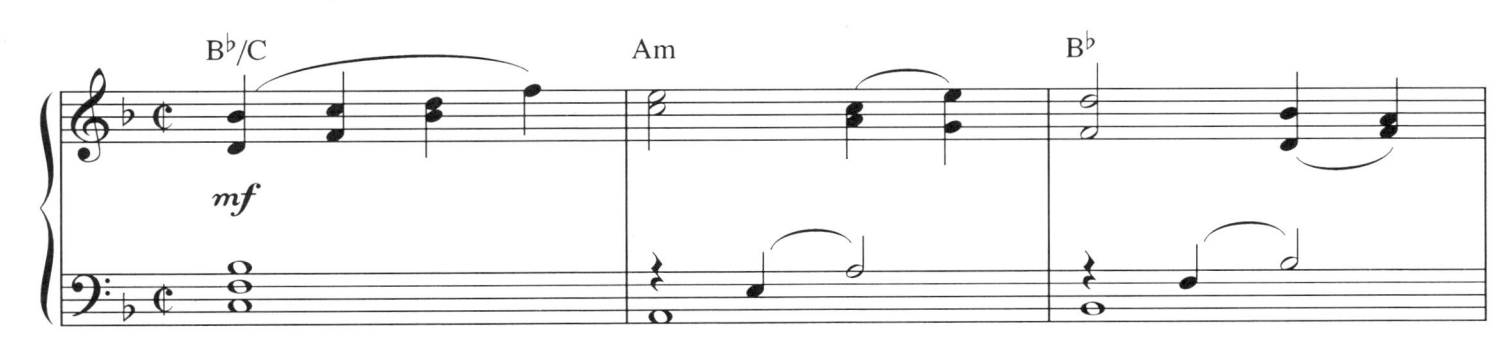

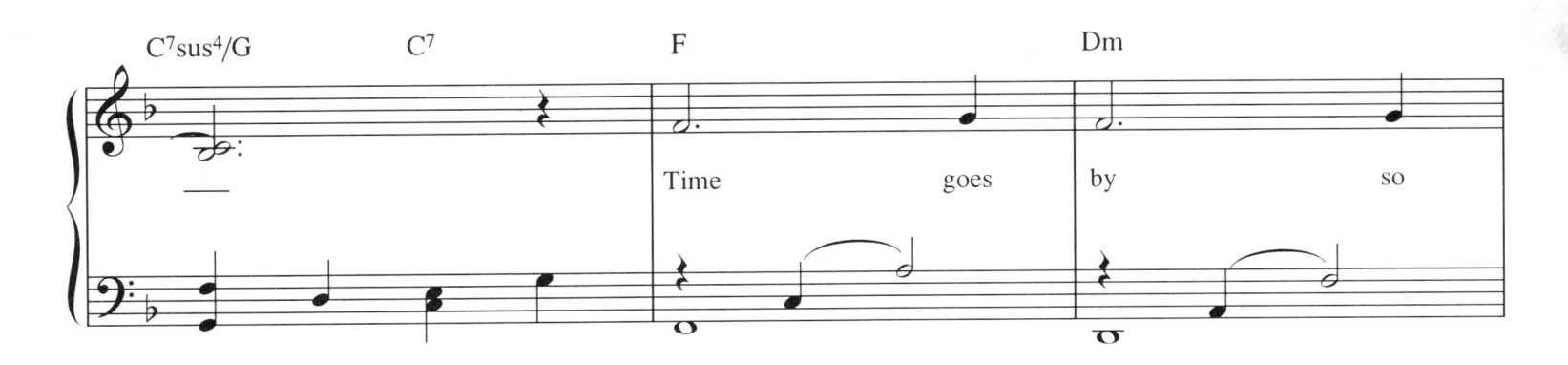

Oh, my love, my dar-ling, I've hun-gered for your touch a long, lone-ly time. Time goes by so

B♭maj7 C7 F
slow - ly and time can do so much, are
Dm Am C7sus4/G C7 F
you still mine? I need your love,
C Dm Am To Coda
I need your love, God
B♭6 Gm7 C7 F
speed your love to me!
B♭ C B♭
1. Lone - ly ri - vers flow to the sea, to the
2. Lone - ly moun - tains gaze at the stars, at the
3
3

A♭ B♭ C7
sea. To the op - en arms of the
stars, Wait - ing for the dawn of the
F B♭ C
sea. Lone - ly ri - vers sigh "Wait for
day. All a - lone I gaze at the
B♭ A♭ B♭ C7
me, wait for me" I'll be com - ing home, wait for
stars, at the stars, Dream - ing of my love far a -
1. F 2. F D.S. al Coda
me. - way.
CODA
B♭6 Gm7 C7 F
speed your love to me!

Up Where We Belong

Words & Music by Jack Nitzsche, Will Jennings & Buffy Sainte Marie

Moderately

Who knows what to-morrow brings; in a world, few hearts sur-vive? All I know is the way I feel; when it's real, I keep it a-live.

Some hang on to "used to be," live their lives look-ing be-hind. All we have is here and now; when all our life, out there to find. The

© Copyright 1982 Famous Music Corporation/Ensign Music Corporation, USA.
All Rights Reserved. International Copyright Secured.

54

road is__ long. There are moun-tains in our way, but we climb a step__ ev-'ry day. Love lift us up where we be - long, where the ea-gles cry on a moun-tain high. Love lift us up where we be - long, far from the world we know;__ up where the clear winds blow.__

D G Gm
dim.
2.
Em9/A A F C E♭ B♭
clear winds blow. Time goes by, no time to cry,
D♭ A♭ B♭ Fm7 B♭7 E♭
Life's you and I, a - live, to - day. Love lift us up where we be -
A♭ Cm Fm E♭ D♭ A♭ B♭
- long, where the ea - gles cry on a moun - tain high.
E♭ A♭ Cm Fm E♭
Love lift us up where we be - long, far from the world we know; up where the

G Cm A♭m E A C♯m
clear winds blow.__ Love lift us up where we be - long, where the
F♯m E D A B E
ea - gles cry on a moun - tain high. Love lift us up where we be -
A C♯m F♯m E
- long, far from the world we know;__ up where the
G♯ C♯m Am E
clear winds blow.__
ff

You'll Never Walk Alone

Music by Richard Rodgers
Words by Oscar Hammerstein II

Moderately

When you walk through a storm, hold your head up high, and don't be a-fraid of the

© Copyright 1949 & 1955 by Richard Rodgers and The Estate of Oscar Hammerstein II. Williamson Music Company owner of publication and allied rights for all countries of the Western Hemisphere and Japan. Williamson Music Limited for all countries of the Eastern Hemisphere (except Japan). This arrangement © Copyright 1998 by Williamson Music Limited, used by Music Sales Limited with permission.
All Rights Reserved. International Copyright Secured.

dark. At the
end of the storm is a
gold - - en sky, and the
sweet sil - ver song of a
lark. Walk

F
Fdim
on through the wind, walk
C
Fm6
C
on through the rain, though your dreams be
C
F
G
tossed and blown. Walk
C
Caug
F
on, walk on, with hope in your
D
C
Caug
heart, and you'll nev - er

Fmaj7 F♯m7(♭5) Em G7
walk a - lone, you'll
C Caug
nev - er
1. F F/G
walk a -
C G
lone. Walk
2. F Dm7 F/G C
walk a - lone.
F C
mp

Wonderful Tonight

Words & Music by Eric Clapton

C D Dsus4 To Coda 1. G
"Yes, you look won-der ful to - night."
"Yes, I feel won-der - ful to - night."
D C D7 Am C D7
2. G C
I feel won - der - ful be -
D Gsus4 G D Em C
- cause I see the love light in your eyes. Then the
D C
won-der of it all is that you just don't re a - lize

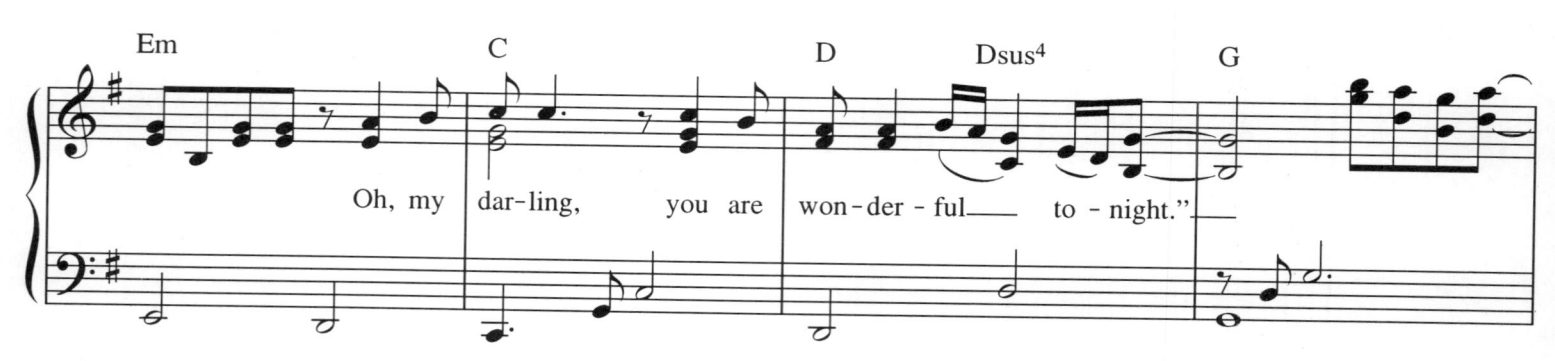

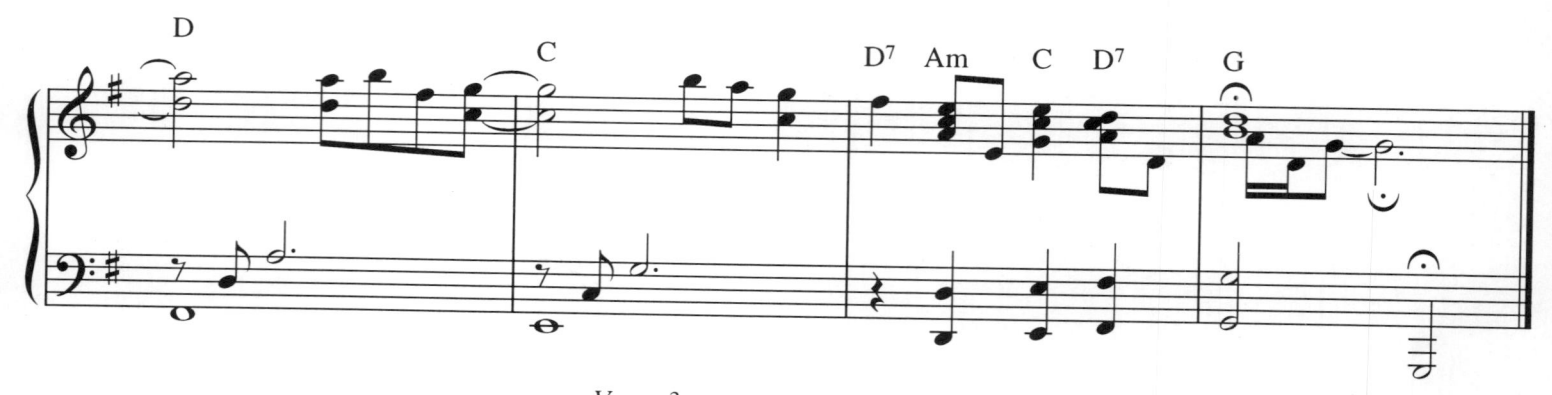

Verse 3:

It's time to go home now,
And I've got an aching head.
So I give her the car keys,
And she helps me to bed.
And then I tell her, as I turn out the light,
I say, "My darling, you are wonderful tonight".